Through the Leaves that Fall

—◊—

GLIMPSES OF GOD
IN THE SEASONS
OF LIFE

MARY EMMA TISINGER

THROUGH THE LEAVES THAT FALL
Glimpses of God in the Seasons of Life
Copyright © 2016 Mary Emma Tisinger
ISBN 978-1-886068-92-6
Library of Congress Control Number 2015960051

Christian Life
Published by Fruitbearer Publishing, LLC
P.O. Box 777, Georgetown, DE 19947
302.856.6649 • FAX 302.856.7742
www.fruitbearer.com • info@fruitbearer.com

Edited by
Melissa Peitsh and Wilma Caraway

Graphic Design by
Candy Abbott

All poetry in this book is by the author with a few exceptions that are noted. The poem, "On Being Behind With One's Reading" as quoted in *SWORD SCRAPBOOK 1*, used with permission by Dr. Shelton L. Smith, President and Editor, Sword of the Lord Ministries.

Scripture quotations marked (KJV) are taken from the Holy Bible, King James Version.

Scripture quotations marked (NIV) are taken from the Holy Bible, New International Version. Copyright © 1973, 1974, 1978, 1984 by International Bible Society. Used by permission of Zondervan Publishing House. All rights reserved.

Scripture quotations marked (RSV) are taken from the Revised Standard Version of the Bible, copyright 1946, 1952, 1971 by the Division of Christian Education of the National Council of Churches of Christ in the USA. Used by permission.

Scripture quotations marked (TLB) are taken from The Living Bible {compter file} Kenneth N. Taylor. electronic ed. Wheaton: Tyndall House, 1997, © 1971 by Tyndale House Publishers, Inc. Used by permission. All rights reserved.

Printed in the United States of America

Dedicated

to

my husband

Ty

in loving memory

—⁓—

Softly they fall,
the leaves of a tree . . .
and the leaves of our lives.
So softly, one might not be aware
that a leaf has fallen;
until later,
long after the experience is over,
we notice the fallen leaf,
understand its significance,
and become aware of God's hand
in our lives.

TABLE OF CONTENTS

—⋙—

A Word to the Reader vii
THE LEAVES OF SPRING 1
The Budding 4
The Wonder of Spring 5
Welcome Guest 6
Here We Go 'Round the Mulberry Bush 7
Golden Morning 9
Little House in the Woods 10
Pine Needles 13
Springtime, Songtime 14
He Who Makes a Garden 16
An Ode to a Spider Web 18
Granddad's Back Porch 19
The Onion Snow 22
Someone Special 23
Covenant 25
Come, Fly With Me 26
I Believe in Spring! 28
THE LEAVES OF SUMMER 31
A Time for Growth 34
Sand Pebbles and Pearls 36
Wonderfully Made 37
You Must Have Been a Beautiful Baby 39
Rules 41
Silent Halls 44
Keeping Balance 45
My God is Real 47
First Kiss 49
Under Protection 50
Like Little Children 51
I Can't Read Cursive Yet 53
Thank God for Change 56
All of Life Is a Weaving 58
THE LEAVES OF FALL 61

Autumn 64
Leaf Mosaic 66
Autumn and the New House 67
A Wonderful Kind of Crazy 70
The Hand That Rocks the Cradle 72
Butterfly Wings 75
Such Love! 76
Birthday Wishes 78
Happy Birthday, Ethan 79
Happy Birthday, Eli 80
I'm Gonna Keep Going 81
I Want to Dance With the Princess 83
Where We Going, Dad? 86
Walking in Faith 89
At the Zoo 90
Seeing With New Eyes 91
The Waiting Room 94
LEAFLESS WINTER 95
The Latter Years 98
January Sand 100
Everywhere, Christmas 101
Bless Me, Too, O My Father 103
Holy Joes 105
Hickory, Dickory, Dock, the Mouse Ran Up the Clock 107
Hold On Tight 108
What Is Lonely? 110
Security 111
Amazing Grace 113
Aftermath 115
In Silhouette 117
What Are You Leaving Behind? 118
Bright Spots 120
Adjusting 124
Some Trust in Chariots 125
Winter Wait 129
In Grateful Appreciation 132
Meet the Author 133
Order Info 135

*"The Leaves of Life keep falling
one by one."*

From
The Rubaiyat of Omar Khayyam
by Omar Khayyam and Edward Fitzgerald

—◊—

A WORD TO THE READER

Persian Poet Omar Khayyam, in his reference to the leaves of life in the book that brought him fame, *The Rubaiyat*, seems to have had the right idea. The leaves of life *do* keep falling.

Just as in nature, God also created us to have our seasons: our spring, our summer, our fall, and our winter. And, as with nature's foliage, each year of our life produces its own crop of leaves—*those unique and varied experiences that help to shape us and determine who we are*—each relevant to, and indicative of, the season.

Like the leaves of a tree—that sprout and bud in the spring, grow and mature through the summer, drop from the tree in the fall, and leave the tree bare in the winter—the leaves of our lives reflect the seasons. Some are mediocre, not very colorful, soon forgotten; yet some are a vibrant red, orange, or yellow—so striking the image lingers. And through it all, God is there.

On the pages of this book, framed in poetry and prose, are brief sketches of the fallen leaves of my life, along with other inspirational pieces. Often encouraged to share my "little stories," this book has been written in the hope that you, the reader, may find something of worth, not only enjoyable to read, but also inspirational and relative to your daily walk.

May you also find glimpses of our Creator, Almighty God, in whose likeness we are formed, whose great love, forgiveness, and promise of tomorrow give meaning to my life. And, I sincerely hope, to yours. It is my prayer that this book may be an encouragement for a closer walk with Him.

Come,
walk with me
through fallen leaves,
remembering
the golden mornings of spring,
the mellowing easy life of summer,
the crispness of autumn,
and winter's winning wisdom.

The Leaves of Spring

—⁓—

Spring

A TIME OF NEWNESS,
BEAUTY,
NEW LIFE,
HOPE,
AND PROMISE

THE BUDDING

God made the early years of our lives like the spring
when the trees begin to bud, the leaves appear,
begin to grow and take shape,
and the buds change to blossoms.

He chooses our parents,
the place we are to be born,
and fashions us in our mother's womb.

Then, at the appointed time
we come into "being"
and
our spring begins.

For you created my inmost being;
you knit me together
in my mother's womb. . . .
My frame was not hidden from you
when I was made in the secret place.
When I was woven together
in the depths of the earth,
your eyes saw my unformed body.
All the days ordained for me
were written in your book
before one of them came to be.
(Psalm 139:13, 15–16 NIV)

THE WONDER OF SPRING

The heavens declare the glory of God;
and the firmament sheweth his handiwork.
(Psalm 19:1 KJV)

B ricusse and Newley have a song entitled, "A Wonderful Day Like Today," which must have been written especially for spring. The words seem so fitting when one sees the new green leaves on shrubs and trees, tulips, daffodils, hydrangea, and flowering shrubs in glorious bloom, and when one catches the fresh, warm fragrance of spring in the air.

God, in His infinite wisdom, must surely have established the seasons as He did—with bright, warm, beautiful spring to follow the drab, bleak coldness of winter—just to renew our hope and to bring us joy. When the signs of spring begin to pop up all around us, let us go down on our knees, as Bricusse and Newley suggest in their song, and give thanks to God—for the wonder of spring!

I will praise you, O Lord, with all my heart;
I will tell of all your wonders.
I will be glad and rejoice in you;
I will sing praise to your name, O Most High.
(Psalm 9:1–2 NIV)

WELCOME GUEST

—∞—

Jonquils are nodding,
forsythia's in bloom;
robins are nesting
and chirping in tune.
Tiny rabbits watch
beneath trembling pines;
spring with its sweetness
has come once again.

HERE WE GO 'ROUND THE MULBERRY BUSH

—⁓—

This is the day which the Lord hath made;
we will rejoice and be glad in it.
(Psalm 118:24 KJV)

It was the last day of school. I had finished first grade, and school was out for the summer. My brother and I ran home, happy to be free again—free from books and lessons and boundaries; free to sleep late, to laugh, and to play. My mother met us at the door, a big smile on her face, her arms open wide.

Later, we ran barefoot across the backyard, around the mulberry tree that stood not too far from the back door. Still "high" on our new-found freedom, we danced in the warm fresh breeze, feeling the squish of the ripe mulberries between our toes, loving the sweet, sweet smell. It was a morning in May—a beautiful golden morning.

Unfortunately, life is not without its troubles and times of unhappiness, but for almost everyone (just as that morning in May was for my brother and me), there are those moments when everything seems to be just as it should be. A time for rejoicing.

—∞—

Thank You, Lord,
for those times in our lives
when we can just "let go,"
and rejoice in You
and Your creation.

GOLDEN MORNING

—∞—

sunshine
painted circles of gold on the window panes
and splashed the sky with golden streaks
in its bright light
the golden crowns of the sunflowers shone

while the little girl with golden curls
skipped happily along the walk
swinging mother's old gold clutch
with its golden chain

she laughed when she saw
the golden wings of the monarch
flutter among the flowers
and ran after him

gold dust fell softly upon her shoes

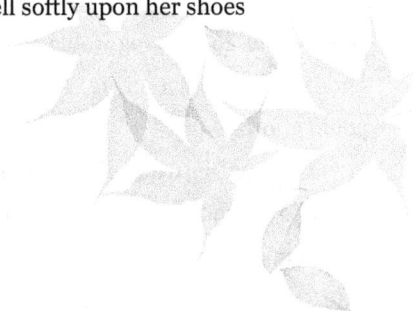

God in His goodness
gave us the wonderful gift of memory.
Our minds are like computers,
storing away everything that happens to us,
to be brought up,
flashed on the screen time after time
and then put back into storage, never to be forgotten.
But, in remembering,
we are also reminded of God's goodness to us,
and of His unfailing love.

—⚎—

Little House in the Woods

I shall never forget our little house in the woods. We moved there when I was six. There were only four rooms, and no running water, but it was home and large enough for the five of us. And probably all my parents could afford.

The road in front of the house was a dirt road, not paved, not even graveled. We were in the woods, so there wasn't much traffic out our way, and the nearest neighbor was a quarter of a mile away. It was quiet and secluded, and I felt secure.

I don't remember ever thinking that we were poor or that our house wasn't as good as other houses—it was just "home" to me. What I liked best was the wonderful area around the house that formed a playground for my brother, sister, and me. There were limits as to how far we could venture, but the area was a treasure trove for us. On a little hill beside the house, there were tall trees with large vine ropes hanging down almost the length of the tree. My brother, sister, and I spent countless hours swinging on those vines, in our little land of make-believe. On the other side of the house, where my father kept his old sedan, trees were spaced just exactly the right distance apart to enable us to create our own little playhouse or secret clubhouse.

What I loved most, though, was my secret room—all my own—down behind the house, under the tall pine trees. I can still see the tiny, beautiful wild violets that grew in the small square formed by the pines.

I could sit, or lie down, on my pine-needle carpet and gaze at the sky through the pine branches high above and wonder about God or admire the tiny violets on the ground around me. No one would bother me.

Sometimes a favorite toy would venture with me into my fairytale world of princesses and gallant knights who rescued them from their captors, before my mother's voice called me back to our ordinary, everyday life in our little house in the woods.

—m—

Remember the days of old;
consider the generations long past.
Ask your father and he will tell you, your elders,
and they will explain to you.
(Deuteronomy 32:7 NIV)

PINE NEEDLES

—⁓—

Violets grew wild there,
a purple surprise
on a pine-needle floor;
trees touched finger tips above.

It wasn't far,
just across the back yard
to the edge of the woods.
Because I was six
I told no one.

I would go there,
hoping not to disturb the "little ones."
If I were lucky
I would feel the brush of their wings
before my mother called.

Sometimes
pine needles stuck to my clothes.

SPRINGTIME, SONGTIME

Who among us has not responded to beautiful music, a beautiful person, a beautiful scene—to all things bright and beautiful?

When I was about thirteen, there was a young lad named Jim, a few years older than I, who lived up the hill. Jim had a beautiful voice, and often, on a gorgeous spring morning, I could hear Jim singing on the hill at the top of his voice. Many times, the words would be a familiar song we sang in school, "Oh, What a Beautiful Morning."

On those occasions, I felt I knew exactly how Jim was feeling and why he was singing—I felt like singing, too. We have within us an inherent appreciation for beauty, placed there by our Creator. God has formed us in such a way that beauty has the ability to flood our souls with joy and cause us to want to burst into song. And, what could be more beautiful than a morning in spring!

Down through the ages, many poets, songwriters, and authors have responded to the beauty of spring. In the Bible, David, the shepherd, must have felt tremendous joy and appreciation for beauty as he tended his father's flocks out on the hillsides. His psalms are full of praise for the beauty that surrounded him. King Solomon, David's son, captured spring's beauty in these words:

> *For, lo, the winter is past,*
> *the rain is over and gone;*
> *The flowers appear on the earth;*
> *the time of the singing of birds is come,*
> *and the voice of the turtle is heard in our land.*
> (Song of Solomon 2:11–12 KJV)

It is beauty, itself, which touches that sensitive spot deep within our souls and allows us to connect instantly with our Creator, who placed it there.

He Who Makes a Garden

*And the Lord God planted a garden eastward in Eden;
and there he put the man whom he had formed.
(Genesis 2:8 KJV)*

In the spring, many people plant flower gardens, and all hope for success. But, have you ever wondered, as I have, why "Contrary Mary" in the old familiar nursery rhyme had such a beautiful garden? The rhyme goes like this:

*Mary, Mary, quite contrary,
How does your garden grow?
With silver bells, and cockle shells,
And pretty maids all in a row.*

Now, I was taught that being contrary was something that should not be rewarded, and it would have made more sense to me if that little rhyme had read:

Mary, Mary, quite contrary,
How does your garden grow?
With dandelions and crab grass,
And ugly weeds all in a row.

Nevertheless, Mary's garden probably grew with "silver bells and cockle shells and pretty maids all in a row" simply because the author felt that gardens should be beautiful.

Beautiful gardens, since the beginning of man, have always been an attraction. The Bible tells us that God made man in His own image and placed him in a beautiful garden, the Garden of Eden. But it seems God did not stop there. He placed within man an appreciation of the beauty of nature, such as we find in a garden, as a link to Himself and a reminder of who He is.

How can one look in the beautiful face of a rose and smell the lovely fragrance; or watch the birds and listen to their song; or sit in the shade of an old oak, stately and magnificent, and not be reminded of the God who created all things? Maltbie Babcock expresses this sentiment in a beautiful old hymn entitled "This Is My Father's World."

The morning light, the lily white, declare their maker's praise. This is my Father's world. His world it is—for all who have eyes to see.

An Ode to a Spider Web

—⚇—

I see the spider web shimmer
among leaves.
Infinity, its name.
Gossamer strands
stretch in all directions;
magic in midair.
I'm awed, enmeshed in wonder.

Yet, how can such beauty
bear two faces,
like a circus clown
with his silly smiles
and unhappy frowns.

The unsuspecting struggles;
snared among sticky strands,
trapped in a silken tangle;
forced to wait
death.

Destroy it?
Destroy such beauty?
Oh, the risks.

Where we live also helps to shape us.
This, too, is part of God's plan.

GRANDDAD'S BACK PORCH

I was born and raised in the mountains of North Carolina. As a child, I liked to visit my grandparents, who lived even farther up in the North Carolina mountains than we did. At Granddad's, it seemed the favorite gathering place was the back porch.

The porch was low, rising about a foot above the surface of the Carolina red clay, dotted here and there with patches of close-cropped green grass. Rectangular in shape, the porch stretched from one end of the bulky old wooden house all the way across the back to Grandma's tiny, aroma-filled kitchen at the other end. A single wooden step, the width of the porch, led up from the ground to the porch floor.

The porch looked old and worn. The long, narrow floorboards were weather-beaten, washed-out, and gray after countless washings by the rain. Those rain baths were sometimes quick, fierce flushes of water thrown forcefully against the wood in a turbulent storm. At other times, the rain fell steadily and quietly on the boards, blown gently in by a lazy wind. The aged boards, once smooth and bright, had become coarse and dull, and in spots the wood seemed weak and crumbly. Countless splinters were hiding there, waiting to stab the delicate bare feet of innocent children who ran disdainfully across them.

On the porch, there were usually several of Granddad's handmade chairs and an old wooden bench pushed up against the wall. The chairs had high, straight backs and checkerboard seats made of strips of cane woven together, resulting in an uncomfortable, rough, pinching surface. The old, brown wooden bench was unquestionably the favored seat for the children.

The breeze, which often glided up the mountainside from the valley below, felt refreshing and cool. Sometimes, as the breeze danced airily across the porch, it carried with it the heavy, sweet smell of honeysuckle, which grew wild and abundantly near the house. Often, the smell it brought was a delicious, tempting aroma of bubbly applesauce, steamy hot bread, or some other equally irresistible aroma from Grandma's kitchen. At other times, especially when the air was damp, the smell was an unwelcome, intruding one, the pungent odor from the nearby cow pasture, pushed rudely into the faces of those who sat on the porch.

From Granddad's back porch, the surrounding grand old mountains looked majestic. They reminded me of God. I often thought they resembled important heads of state gathered around a conference table to make a momentous decision. The myriad assortment of trees upon them gave a nubby texture to their appearance, which changed in color depending upon the time of day and the weather. Under the noonday sun, they were a hot, bright green. When the rain fell and the sky was overcast, the mountains looked dark and gray. In the evening, as the fiery red sun stooped lower and lower behind them, they donned royal garments of blue and purple, shadowed here and there with darker hues of blue and gray.

Occasionally, the lonely melancholy tinkle of a cowbell could be heard in the distance. Sometimes, the quiet was interrupted by the barking of an unidentified dog giving an excited warning to someone or something. Often, at dusk, a wise, curious old friend in the woods would call out his oft-repeated, always unanswerable question, "Who? Whooo?"

Father,
Thank You for loving us so much that You place,
not only special people in our lives,
but also special places
that hide in our hearts.

THE ONION SNOW

Forsythia, flanked by holly,
stands tall,
gold and green against the snow.
On the roof, a mockingbird sings.

Evergreens greet the dawn,
as graceful gulls glide
through the cold, gray sky.

Sparrows dart here, then there.
Nervous,
they search for food
while starlings watch
from the pin oak across the way.

On the snow-covered lawn a robin rests.
He knows the snow,
dropped lightly on the ground
like Grandma's coverlet,
won't last long.

"It's the onion snow," Grandpa says,
"We'll have onions soon."

SOMEONE SPECIAL

The hoary head is a crown of glory,
if it be found in the way of righteousness.
(Proverbs 16:31 KJV)

God places special people in our lives. To my childish eyes, my granddad was an imposing figure. He was tall—taller than anyone else I knew—a giant, big and strong. With his gray hair, and steely eyes that could bore a hole right through you, one instinctively knew that he was the one in charge. And when he spoke, we children knew we did not dare disobey. Even Grandma did what he said, and Momma and Daddy listened to him. The fact that he walked with a cane only made him seem that much more authoritative. Once, when he whacked my cousin with his cane, I determined I did not want that to happen to me. So when Granddad spoke, I listened carefully.

Granddad was accustomed to having others listen when he spoke. Retired, he had served the county where he lived as a deputy sheriff. I liked to look at the old photographs in which he wore his sheriff's badge and gun, and wonder about his experiences with those who broke the law. But he never talked about it.

Granddad was good with his hands. It seemed he was always whittling on a piece of wood, working on something. He made all kinds of wooden puzzles, and often, when a neighbor would come to visit, one would see them striving to outdo each other with one of the puzzles. The back porch bore evidence of his handiwork, too, in the many sturdy, handmade wooden chairs pushed up against the wall. I often wondered if Granddad made the old wooden bench that the children always scrambled to sit on, but I never asked.

One hot, summer day in July, Granddad had a visitor. He took him down to the spring, a little ways from the house, and brought out one of his bottles of homemade root beer that he kept in the spring to keep cold. That day, he let my sister, brother, and me tag along, and let us sample the root beer. Such a wonderful taste! I wondered why Granddad had never mentioned it, or let us have any before, but I didn't dare ask why. That seemed to be another one of those things the grown-ups didn't talk about, and no one ever questioned. It was much later that I learned that the mountain Granddad lived on was well known as a haunt for bootleggers with their illegal stills and moonshine whiskey. That knowledge only made me wonder even more about Granddad's "little spring" down below the house.

As I grew, we made that trip up into the mountains less often, and one day we received word that Granddad had passed away. I was sad, and the old house seemed lonely and forlorn when we arrived. Granddad was always, and forever will be, in my memories, someone very special.

COVENANT

All I could see from where I stood
were branches,
leaves trembling.
Flags bowed
their reds, yellows, and greens
against a silent sky.
Birds on familiar paths
among tall trees,
sang.

A promise of tomorrow.

COME, FLY WITH ME

If I take the wings of the morning,
and dwell in the uttermost parts of the sea;
Even there shall thy hand lead me,
and thy right hand shall hold me.
(Psalm 139:9–10 KJV)

With spring comes the month of March—the windy month. Often, when March arrives, I find myself watching to see if the old adage, *when March comes in like a lamb, it will go out like a lion,* or vice versa, holds true. Often, I have found that it does. But, I have also seen that March truly deserves its name, "the windy month."

Wind—It can be gentle and quiet, barely noticeable in the outdoors on quiet spring days. Or, it can be noisy, strong and forceful, sometimes quite damaging to anything in its path. The powerful force of a tornado, leaves blown from the trees, and kites flying high in the sky all speak of the wind. But, whatever its nature on any particular day— the wind speaks of God.

I cannot watch the young-at-heart fly their kites without being reminded of God. The kites—so colorful, so graceful—dip and soar, fly high or low, depending upon the wind. We are like the kites. Each of us is different. We may be different in color, different in abilities, different in size and shape. Some of us are tall, some short; some wide, some thin, just as we were created by God. And, like the kites, some of us fly higher in life than others, some lower. Some of us manage to stay lifted up for long periods of time, while some seem barely able to stay up at all, remaining afloat for only a brief period of time before coming down. Even the coming-down process can be different—some come down slowly and gracefully, while others seem to tumble, or drop with a thud to the ground.

What is the unseen force that lifts us up and makes us soar like the kites? Our wind is the breath of God. It is He who lifts us up. He holds us steady on our course, or carries us where He would have us go. He sustains us and enables us to achieve His plan for our lives, and so, to bear witness for Him.

Come, fly with me. Let us enjoy the winds of March, and give praise to God.

I Believe in Spring!

Thou hast put gladness in my heart.
(Psalm 4:7a KJV)

Spring, with its familiar signs of new life—tiny crocuses pushing up through the earth, daffodils and forsythia in bloom, trees budding, birds nesting, baby bunnies hopping across the lawn—is a source of joy. One can often hear such happy phrases as, "Oh, my crocuses are up," or, "My daffodils are blooming!"

Sometimes, however, just when we decide that spring is truly on its way, along comes a big snow storm or a cold spell that sends thoughts of spring running for cover.

Many of us can remember a late March or an April snow, awaking in the morning to the sound of birds singing outside the bedroom, and then throwing open the drapes only to see a white world outside. A world of snow. But, we can still believe in spring.

We can believe in spring for we have our loving heavenly Father's promise in these words in the Bible: *While the earth remaineth, seedtime and harvest, and cold and heat, and summer and winter, and day and night shall not cease.* (Genesis 8:22 KJV). So, we can be sure that season will follow season, cycle will follow cycle, not just in nature—but in all of life.

When my children were small, I taught them to sing "When the Red, Red Robin Comes Bob, Bob, Bobbin' Along." One day, my daughter Lisa, who is grown now and at the time was in her first or second year of teaching first grade, called to say, "Oh, Mom, guess what I taught my kids today?" I had no idea.

"I taught them to sing 'When the Red, Red Robin Comes Bob, Bob, Bobbin' Along'. They are so cute," she said, "twenty-eight little heads all bobbing up and down."

I could just picture it, and wasn't I pleased! To think that something I had done years ago had made an impression and was being passed on. Yes, I believe in spring!

—∞—

Ah, that's the reason a bird can sing—
On his darkest day he believes in spring.

—Douglas Malloch

The Leaves of Summer

Summer

—〰—

A Time for Growing, Maturing, and Bearing Fruit

A Time for Growth

Just as the leaves of spring parallel the early years of our lives, the leaves of summer mark the middle years of our existence. God made the period from young adulthood through the middle years of one's life a time for continued growth, maturing, and bearing fruit—according to His divine plan.

These words from an old, familiar song, "In the Good Old Summer Time," give an adequate description of summer for many of us. Most see summer as generally a happy, more relaxed, good and pleasant time of the year. The weather is warm, the world is green and flowery with verdant growth, beautiful and pleasant, abuzz with life. So, it seems, is the summer of our lives. Summer is the time when we emerge from our cocoon of childhood, to try our wings and fly out into the world of adults. It is the time in which we continue to grow and mature, through college and career, marriage and family; the time in which we establish our identity and find our place in the world.

But, who can say when it is we cross that threshold from childhood into young adulthood? In nature, we have definite dates to mark the beginning of each season. In our lives, however, there is no definite line of demarcation separating one period of growth from the next, and our experiences overlap, according to our own individual, God-given timetable.

But we grow,
and as we grow,
each life-experience helps to shape us
and determine who we are to become.

—⁂—

The steps of a good man are ordered by the Lord:
and he delighteth in his way.
(Psalm 37:23 KJV)

SAND PEBBLES AND PEARLS

In the sand by the sea
children play,
searching for treasures swept in by the tides
moving steadily,
rhythmically,
naturally, noisily,
onto the shore.

"Listen and hear,"
says the conch,
"the roar of the ocean
when I'm held to your ear."
"Pick me up gently,"
speaks the clam of his shell.
"This is my home, it has served me well."

While the starfish reveals
its stellar star shape,
the oyster waits quietly
his secret to tell,
that the pearl he holds
is rare and as dear
as silver and gold.

Hardly noticed,
the sand pebble shines in the sun,
smoothed and refined by water and time
as the tides rush in
and slowly recede,
leaving their treasures
in the sand by the sea.

WONDERFULLY MADE

The great musician Wolfgang Amadeus Mozart, it is said, once overheard a certain young man play the piano and commented, "He will give the world something worth listening to." Mozart's prediction came true. This young man, Ludwig van Beethoven, became one of the greatest composers in musical history.

It is interesting, though, that Beethoven began to lose his hearing when he was in his twenties, and later became deaf. Yet his deafness did not hinder his composing; he continued to write music. Many are familiar with his famous fifth symphony, *Eroica*; or perhaps his ninth, *Pastorale*, or the opera, *Fidelio*.

However, I cannot help but wonder, how could he write music when he could not hear? The answer must lie in the fact that music had become such a part of Beethoven's soul that he no longer needed physical ears to hear the notes.

What a great God we have—to create us in such an amazing, wonderful way. We can say with the psalmist these words of praise:

*I will praise thee; for I am fearfully
and wonderfully made:
marvelous are thy works; and that
my soul knoweth right well.*
(Psalm 139:14 KJV)

You Must Have Been a Beautiful Baby

But the Lord said to Samuel,
"Do not consider his appearance
or his height, for I have rejected him.
The Lord does not look at the things man looks at."
(1 Samuel 16:7a NIV)

I have often thought that God must make babies beautiful, sweet, and innocent so that we cannot help but love them and want to take care of them. But, babies have a way of growing up, and as they grow, they usually change—inwardly and outwardly.

I read an article once about Lorraine Bracco, beautiful star of the movie, *Someone to Watch Over Me.* In the article, Lorraine recounted living in Brooklyn as a child, and being sort of a "tomboy." When she was ten, the family moved to Long Island. This meant attending a new school where, according to Lorraine, the other girls were stylish and wore clothes from Saks Fifth Avenue, while she said she had no sense of style. But more traumatic was the day on the school bus when the other girls took a vote and voted her the most unattractive girl on the bus.

Deeply hurt, Lorraine said she went home that day, sat on her father's lap and cried and cried. Eventually, with her father's help, she came to understand that real beauty lies within, that no matter how the other girls treated her, she could be pretty inside. And—in God's eyes, that's what counts, isn't it?

—⁘—

"Man looks at the outward appearance,
but the Lord looks at the heart."
(1 Samuel 16:7b NIV)

Rules

Rules, it seems, are a necessary evil. We don't like to be bound by them, but history and experience have shown that living with others necessitates the making of rules.

We have our rules of logic; our *Robert's Rules of Order*. We have our constitutions, including the Constitution of the United States of America, and our Bill of Rights. We have our laws, our by-laws, our handbooks, Emily Post's *Rules of Etiquette*, Dr. Benjamin Spock, and other guidelines.

However, man's rules are not perfect, and often need to be revised or amended. Some may even need to be done away with, as the author of the following poem implies:

> Junior bit the meter man.
> Junior kicked the cook.
> Junior's antisocial now
> (according to the book).

Junior smashed the clock and lamp.
Junior hacked the tree.
(Destructive trends are treated
in chapters two and three.)

Junior threw his milk at mom.
Junior screamed for more.
(Notes on self-assertiveness
are found in chapter 4.)

Junior got in Grandpop's room,
tore up his fishing line;
that's to gain attention.
(See page 89.)

Grandpop seized a slipper and
yanked Junior 'cross his knee.
(Grandpa hasn't read a book
since 1893.)

—Selected, "On Being Behind with One's Reading,"
The Sword Scrapbook I.

So much for man's guidelines. But, there is one book
of guidelines we do not want to throw away—God's book—
the Bible. God's laws never need revising, and they come
with a promise.

Psalm 19 reads:

The law of the Lord is perfect, converting the soul: the testimony of the Lord is sure, making wise the simple.

The statutes of the Lord are right, rejoicing the heart: the commandment of the Lord is pure, enlightening the eyes.

. . . the judgments of the Lord are true and righteous altogether.

More to be desired are they than gold, yea, than much fine gold:

Moreover by them is thy servant warned: and in keeping of them there is great reward.

(Psalm 19:7, 8, 9b, 10a & 11 KJV)

—⁂—

Almighty God, teach us your way. Amen.

SILENT HALLS

—ɷ—

Silent, the noisy halls
where school bells rang,
shadows of the mind;
once they teemed with hopes and dreams
of exuberant youth,
like the open sky—endless, unconfined.
The pot of gold at rainbow's end
was already ours;
our youth—our stimulus, elixir, and cause.

Tassels tossed, we raced to life,
to goals, success;
with dreams of marriage, happiness;
some college-bound,
some to careers,
our finite minds—our only bounds.

Expectations of yesteryear are memories now,
treasured moments sculpt by Time,
who tiptoed by with slippered feet,
unnoticed;
until the day we realized
youth had gone
and we remained behind.

We're wiser now,
ensconced in truth,
revealed by time,
suppressed by youth,
that life holds both the good and bad—
and all things change.

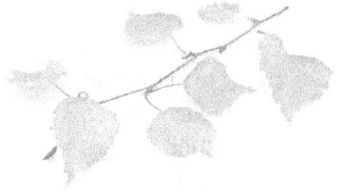

KEEPING BALANCE

*But seek ye first the kingdom of God
and His righteousness;
and all these things shall be added unto you.*
(Matthew 6:33 KJV)

Are there days when you feel you just don't have time for God? When it seems there's so much to do that you just can't take time to read your Bible and spend a few minutes in prayer? I must confess, I have had those days.

Life is a matter of balance. We need to balance the hours of rest we get at night with the hours of activity we have during the day. We need to balance the amount of food we consume each day—eat the right foods (enough to be healthy), but not overeat. We have to balance work with recreation, exercise against inactivity, and calories against nourishment. We need to allow time for ourselves, time for our family, and most importantly, time for God. That's a lot of balancing! But, this old world just keeps on turning, and we keep on struggling to maintain our balance.

Sometimes when life becomes rather hectic, and I'm trying to fit too many "things" into the hours God has given me for each day, I am reminded of the Scriptures and what we are told is most important. I remember Jesus' visit to Mary and Martha, and how Martha busied herself with hostess duties while Mary sat at Jesus' feet and listened to His teaching. When Martha complained and asked Jesus to tell Mary she should help her, Jesus' answer was illuminating:

Martha, Martha,
thou art careful and troubled about many things:
But one thing is needful:
and Mary hath chosen that good part,
which shall not be taken away from her.
(Luke 10:41–42 KJV)

Needless to say, when we put God first, everything else just seems to fall into place!

—///—

Almighty God,
Help me to remember that life
is all about You.
Help me to choose, always,
that good part
which shall not be taken away.

My God Is Real

During my "growing up" teenage years, there was a popular religious song that I loved and would sing over and over. The words of the song, *My God is real, for I can feel Him in my soul,* spoke to me. I loved the melody and I loved the words. They ran through my mind over and over, and I would find myself singing the song again and again. I had become a Christian and was involved in a church—and God **was** real to me.

But now that I am older, I am able to look back and see that the God that was real to me then is not the same as the God I know today.

Why? Has God changed? *No.* God is everlasting, unchanging—the same yesterday, today, and forever. *But I have changed.* Through the years that have passed, I have gotten to know Him better and have grown closer to Him. Through spending time with Him in Bible study and prayer, through worship and fellowship with other believers, through serving Him, and leaning upon Him through life's trials, my roots have grown deeper and deeper into Christ and I have grown spiritually.

Today, the words, *My God is real, for I can feel Him in my soul,* ring with truth as never before.

—∞—

And now just as you trusted Christ to save you . . .
Live in vital union with him.
Let your roots grow down into him and draw up
nourishment from him.
See that you go on growing in the Lord.
(Colossians 2:6-7 TLB)

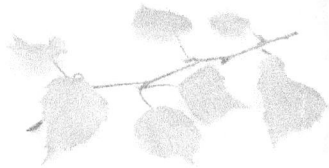

FIRST KISS

The church behind us
and the trees around
were shadows in the night,
framed in the glow of snowflakes,
lacy, white.
The air was hushed and still
as softly they fell,
and softer yet, caressed my face,
upturned, in wonder and delight.
When suddenly you leaned
your face so close to mine
and gently pressed your lips
against my mouth,
snowflake light.
It was only a moment
in the treasury of time,
but just enough to seal completely
the ethereal sweetness
forever
in my mind.

—◊—

Set me as a seal upon thine heart,
as a seal upon thine arm:
for love is strong as death.
(Song of Solomon 8:6 KJV)

UNDER PROTECTION

For thou hast been my help,
and in the shadow of thy wings I sing for joy.
(Psalm 63:7 RSV)

It was mid-afternoon. I waited at a large, busy intersection on the edge of town for the light to change from red to green. Suddenly, two birds high up in the sky above the intersection caught my attention. The smaller of the two seemed to be having difficulty flying and appeared to be falling. Quickly, the larger bird moved directly beneath the smaller one to break its fall. Wings fluttering, the smaller bird again attempted to fly while the larger hovered near, circling around, above and beneath it. I realized then—it was a mother bird teaching her young how to fly.

How like our God, I thought. He waits nearby, always ready to help, to move near and break our fall—not only when we spread our wings and attempt to fly, but at all times. Truly, as the psalmist says, He covers us with His feathers, and under His wings we find refuge.

Thank You, God,
for Your promise to be always near,
watching over us. Amen.

Printed previously in *The Secret Place*, Fall 1996, American Baptist Churches in the U.S.A.

Like Little Children

One afternoon our daughter, son-in-law, and one-and-only little grandson, Anthony, came to visit. I rushed to greet them, and opened the door which leads to the garage. Anthony was standing just outside the garage, but he didn't see me. Waiting patiently while his mother removed some things from the car, I heard him say, "Momma, what are Granddad and Mom-Mom doing?"

"I don't know," she replied. "Why don't you go in and find out?"

Just then, Anthony looked over and saw me. His face beamed, and he ran toward me as fast as his two-and-a-half-year-old legs could run.

We can learn so much from little children. Anthony, so eager to come inside, was hesitant and wanted assurance that it would be all right. He didn't know that I had been watching and waiting for him, and that I wanted to see him just as much as he wanted to see me . . . probably even more. What joy for both of us—when his face lit up with a big smile, so did mine—as we rushed to greet each other.

God waits for us, longs for us, to come to Him—just as I waited for Anthony, with eagerness and anticipation. He knows our hearts; He knows our desires, our thoughts. He knows our words before they are even spoken. Our desire to see Him, our going to Him, surely gives Him joy, just as Anthony's desire to see his granddad and mom-mom brought joy to us. We are made in our heavenly Father's image—imagine God's joy when you or I, like a little child, "run" to Him with a big smile upon our face.

Suffer little children to come unto me,
and forbid them not:
for of such is the kingdom of God.
(Luke 18:16 KJV)

I Can't Read Cursive Yet

But each man has his own gift from God;
one has this gift, another has that.
(1 Corinthians 7:7 NIV)

Peter was in my third grade class in Sunday School. His father had been stationed at the Air Force Base in Dover for a number of years but was now being transferred to Germany. Soon Peter and his family would be moving there.

On Peter's last day in class, I had a present for him—a miniature of a well-known painting of a young boy on a boat in the midst of a terrible storm. In the picture, the sky is black, the rain is pouring down, and the wind and waves are tossing the boat to and fro while the water splashes mightily onto the deck. The boy struggles to hold on to the steering wheel and guide the boat, and his face shows his anxiety and the stress of the situation. However, standing just behind the boy is Jesus, reaching around the boy, his hands on the boat's steering wheel. He is helping the boy keep control of the boat. This picture, I knew, would be the perfect gift for Peter.

Attached to the gift was a card on which I had written a few sentences, telling Peter that this gift was a reminder for him that no matter how far away he moved, no matter where he was, Jesus would always be with him. I meticulously chose my words. Words I hoped would impress Peter so much he would never forget them, or me, or the class.

At the appropriate time, I presented the gift to Peter. When he opened the card, I waited eagerly for his reaction, but there was none. He simply stood there, looking at the card, the gift unopened in his hands. "Peter," I said, "why don't you read the card to the others?"

Looking upset, Peter glanced at me. "But I can't read cursive yet."

So then, I read the card to Peter and the class, and Peter opened his gift. He was pleased—but I was disappointed. The message on the card was an important part of the gift, which, I thought, would make the gift more meaningful to Peter when he read the words. But I had not taken into consideration the fact that Peter might not be able to read cursive writing, and so he remained standing—with an unopened gift in his hands. The incident was one I have never forgotten.

God gives to each of us talents and abilities, which some call "gifts." Some have been given musical talents— the ability to sing, perhaps, or play a musical instrument, even to compose music. Some have been given the ability to write—poetry, articles, dramas, stories—for others to read and enjoy. Some have the ability to draw, to paint beautiful pictures; some can design and sew beautiful garments. There are many different kinds of gifts, and these gifts are meant to be "opened," used, and shared with others.

Each one should use whatever gift he has received
to serve others,
faithfully administering God's grace
in its various forms.
(1 Peter 4:10 NIV)

—∙∙∙—

Lord,
Help me not to disappoint You, by holding
your gifts "unopened" in my hands.
Grant that I may use them
to show your love to others.
Amen.

THANK GOD FOR CHANGE

Early in our marriage, my husband and I moved to Delaware.

Delaware:
the "First State," the "small wonder,"
home of the lady bug and the famous Blue Hen,
home of the holly and the pine;
God's Country!

But, moving to a place so flat, after living in the mountains of North Carolina, was just too much for me. I did not like Delaware; I did not like . . .

the flatness;
the tall, narrow two-story houses
that stood by the side of the road
with surrounding fields that stretched on . . .
and on . . . and on;
the mosquitoes;
the odor of the swamp;
the mosquito-sprayer plane that zoomed low,
spreading its fumes;
the smell of fertilizer on a warm day
that took one's breath away;
the lonely cry of seagulls circling overhead;

the sound of engines revving up
at Dover Air Force Base
at two o'clock in the morning;
the wind that seemed to blow continuously.

—◌◌—

But, after a while, things began to change. I changed. I came to love . . .

the flatness;
the tall, narrow two-story houses
that stood by the side of the road
with fields that stretched on,
and on, and on . . . surrounding;
the smell of fertilizer on a warm day
that took one's breath away;
the distinctive odor of the swamp;
the lonely cry of seagulls circling gracefully overhead;
the sound of engines revving up
at Dover Air Force Base
at two o'clock in the morning;
the wind that seemed to blow continuously.

And now, I thank God for Delaware. I thank God for change, for the ability to adjust, for growth, for the realization that without change there is no growth. But most of all, I thank God for the fact that He never changes. He's always the same, yesterday, today, and tomorrow. And—His great love endures forever.

ALL OF LIFE IS A WEAVING

Like the weaver's thread
when cast on the loom
is the birth of a child,
a tapestry's begun.
All of life is a weaving.

Like the warp and the weft,
our lives intertwine with those around us
in marvelous design.
Father and mother, and varied kin
mix and mingle and draw us in
to a maze of angles
and ups and downs.

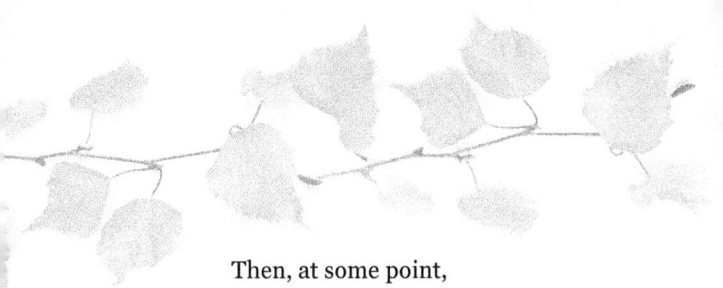

Then, at some point,
our lives diverge;
the fabric widens and colors merge.
There's husband or wife,
job associates, too;
neighbors, and friends, and strangers who
may touch our lives as the shuttle moves.
All of life is a weaving.

Greatly blessed is he
who sees the design is the work of the Master,
our Creator divine;
who gives life
and molds the form we take;
then fashions the path our lives shall make,
as we weave the threads He places on the loom,
'til the task is complete
and the tapestry's done.
All of life is a weaving.

All of life is a weaving.

The Leaves of Fall

Autumn

—⚶—

A Time for Harvest,
for Gathering In
And
Enjoying
The Fruits of One's Labor

Autumn

Fall, or autumn, the time for harvest, is a showcase prepared by our Creator—a collage of red, yellow, and orange—evident in the foliage around us as we walk through our yards, drive down the street, or travel a country road. We see the touch of His artist's brush in the fields of harvested corn, the shocks neatly rolled up into bundles, and in the golden glow of pumpkins, heavy on the vine. We can feel the warmth of His love as we bite into a red delicious apple, or enjoy the wonderful fragrance of apple or pumpkin pie, filtering through the kitchen.

In similar fashion,

God uses His artist's brush upon us,

so that the autumn of our lives

might also be bright and colorful,

fruitful and satisfying . . .

If we but listen to His voice,

and remain

obedient and faithful.

—⁓—

Blessed is the man
who does not walk in the counsel of the wicked . . .
But his delight is in the law of the Lord,
and on his law he meditates day and night.
He is like a tree planted by streams of water,
which yields its fruit in season
and whose leaf does not wither.
Whatever he does prospers.
(Psalm 1:1–3 NIV)

LEAF MOSAIC

Slightly crumpled,
they lay on the shiny wet surface
of the walkway,
red, orange, yellow, brown,
and a few green.

Tossed carelessly down
by the unruly winds
of the night's Nor'easter,
they had paused to rest
on the chocolaty-brown,
freshly-painted boards
beneath my feet.

Strokes of the brush
of the Master Artist,
God.
And only God.

AUTUMN AND THE NEW HOUSE

I had just started fifth grade when we moved into our new house. There was a coolness in the air—the crispiness of autumn was all around. Crispiness. The word always brings back memories—memories of dry, stiff leaves that drop from the trees in the fall; leaves that break easily and crumble into pieces beneath one's feet; pumpkins resting lazily on the vine, with their firm orange shells; and crunchy, firm apples. And how can one forget the crisp autumn air with its cool, dry feel that called for a sweater in the morning, which one slipped off in the warmth of the noon-day sun and donned again in the evening? And, the new house.

There were five of us: Momma, Daddy, my older brother, my younger sister, and I, in the house on Drum's Straight. I loved that house right from the beginning. We were on the main highway, a long, straight stretch of land that obviously belonged at one time to someone named Drum. Compared to the little four-room house we had been living in, the new house was a rich man's dwelling. And, this one was out of the woods. We were out in the open, free from the trees that had towered over our former little house and formed a circle around us, to shelter us. Or, could it have been—to imprison us?

I shall always remember the feeling that crowded into my heart, leaving no room for anything else, the day we moved to Drum's Straight, and I walked into the new home. We went there from school the day our parents moved our belongings into the house. It was a fall afternoon. The sun shone through the living room windows onto the bare wooden floor. My, it was beautiful. The bareness added to its beauty. The little cracker-box room that had been ours, quite crowded with five people, could not compare to the large, new living room with its big windows and a front door that was mostly glass. The windows, the door, the room, all seemed to say, "Hello! Come in and stay awhile; you're going to love it here!"

And, I did. I loved the crispiness of the air, the smell of wood smoke, the scent of leaves burning over on the hill in the distance, the way the sun cast shadows as it began to set in the western sky. I loved the sound of my mother's voice as she called us inside to begin our homework or to eat supper. Somehow, the crispiness would follow us in. It lingered while we ate; sat beside us as we did our homework; and crawled into bed with us when it was time. Yes, that must be the way it seeped into my soul as I slept and became a part of me that would never be forgotten—a forever reminder of the new house and the falling leaves of autumn.

The God who made the world and everything in it,
being Lord of heaven and earth,
does not live in shrines made by man,
nor is he served by human hands,
as though he needed anything,
since he himself gives to all men life and breath
and everything.
And he made from one every nation of men
to live on all the face of the earth,
having determined allotted periods and
the boundaries of their habitation . . .
(Acts 17:24–26 RSV)

A WONDERFUL KIND OF CRAZY

Use hospitality one to another without grudging.
(1 Peter 4:9 KJV)

One evening, my husband and I were invited to a dinner party given by friends who are in the antique business. Their home is filled with antiques—beautiful treasures. About thirty guests had been invited, and the hostess presented all sorts of hot dishes, cold salads, various kinds of breads and numerous desserts; and she had done all the preparation herself. As I looked around at all the food, I remembered the times I have entertained—and all the work involved in getting the house in shape and the food ready.

I was so amazed to see all the work my friend had done, I told her so. She only smiled and said, "Crazy aren't I?"

I responded with the first words that came to my mind, "Yes, but it's a wonderful kind of crazy."

Since then, I've thought a lot about that evening, and that friend. Knowing that my friend had gone to so much trouble to have her house guest-ready—inviting, clean, and attractive—made me feel very special. And, I am sure the other guests must have felt the same way. It seemed obvious that, although her house was full of beautiful antiques, the antiques were not "most important" in her life. My friend truly cared about others.

I left the party that evening, inspired to try to be more like my friend—more caring of others, more willing to serve, more willing to be "a wonderful kind of crazy."

THE HAND THAT ROCKS THE CRADLE

American poet William Ross Wallace is best known for his poem, "The Hand that Rocks the Cradle Is the Hand that Rules the World."

Now, William Ross Wallace was born in 1819 and died in 1891, so we can feel rather certain that the hand to which he was referring would be that of a woman. In today's twenty-first century society, however, we could not be sure, for today we have our "Mr. Moms," husbands who, for various reasons, have chosen to stay home with the kids while the wife goes to work. Regardless of whose hand it is that rocks the cradle, it seems that Wallace was really saying—it is women who rule the world.

It is true that mothers do have tremendous influence in shaping the lives of their children, and it has also been observed that wives can, and do, influence their husbands—even those in leadership positions. Today, more and more women are assuming leadership roles in the working world, in government, and in all walks of life. However, all things considered, while it is debatable as to whether women actually rule the world, it seems to be true that women do play an important role in what is happening in the world.

Ever since biblical days, women have been leaders in society. Deborah was a biblical leader. She was a prophetess and a judge. Lydia was a business woman, a seller of purple; Esther saved the Jewish people from being destroyed; Miriam, the sister of Moses, was considered to be a leader among the Israelites. Down through the ages, women have been seen in leadership positions.

What makes a person, whether man or woman, a good leader? There are many characteristics that could be cited: integrity, honesty, loyalty, willingness to listen, compassion . . . the list is long. But probably, one of the most important is illustrated in the following story, which was told to me by a friend, of a little girl who was obviously a leader:

A little girl was upset because her brother set a trap to catch birds.

She wept at first but then her mother noticed she was cheerful again.

When asked about her cheerfulness, she said, "I prayed for my brother to be a better boy,

and I prayed that the trap would not catch any
more birds."

"What else?" asked the mother.

"Then I went out and kicked the trap to pieces."

This little anecdote (author unknown) is supposed
to make us smile, but it also bears an important point for
everyone. Before taking action, the little girl *prayed first*.
She had been influenced (by someone) to seek the Lord's
guidance about matters before taking action. This alone
could play an important role in shaping one's life, that of
others, and possibly *the world*.

—៣—

Trust in the Lord with all thine heart;
and lean not unto thine own understanding.
In all thy ways acknowledge Him,
and He shall direct thy paths.
(Proverbs 3:5–6 KJV)

BUTTERFLY WINGS

(On the birth of our first grandchild)

It was love that I held in my arms today,
tiny, pink, asleep and still;
love born of love,
a gift of new life,
as butterfly wings hovered near.

There were traces of pollen
in baby-fine hair,
tiny fingers curled around mine.
It was the future, I knew,
holding onto the past,
as butterfly wings fluttered by.

For I knew in my heart
winter surely would come,
but my arms held the promise of spring . . .
that flowers will bloom
again and again
with the touch of butterfly wings.

Such Love!

If God so loved us,
we also ought to love one another.
(1 John 4:11 RSV)

My mother has been gone for a number of years now, but I can still see her. After I married and moved out of state, each time I returned home for a visit, it was always the same. As I drove up, I could see her through the living room window, hurrying toward the door. In a moment or two, the door would open and she would appear, a beautiful smile on her face, her arms opened wide, as she rushed to greet me. Her hug was always tight, warm, and loving. That has become my most vivid remembrance of her—how much she loved me!

Jesus told the parable of the prodigal son (Luke 15:11–20) to help us understand how much our heavenly Father loves us. In the story, the father saw his son coming and, overjoyed, could not wait, but ran to meet him—as my mother did for me. The Bible, however, tells us that God's love for us is greater by far than ours for our children could ever be. He gave His only son to die on the cross in order that we might live.

For God so loved the world,
that he gave his only begotten son,
that whosoever believeth in him should not perish,
but have everlasting life.
(John 3:16 KJV)

How much He loves us!

Heavenly Father,
Help me to so love my children
that it may bear witness to them of your great love.
Amen.

Published previously in *The Secret Place,* Fall 1996,
American Baptist Churches in the U.S.A.

BIRTHDAY WISHES

Little boy, upon my knee,
you were two, and now you're three.
Tell me, please, what dreams we'll find
you hold within your tender mind?

Are Tigger and Pooh, and Christopher Robin
waiting to play?
Or is Tommy the Train
chugging along the tracks today?

Is there a Big Rig,
or a trip to Granddad's,
with a dollar for the "Bear,"
and a lollipop red?

Oh, it's a magical land,
that place in your mind
where dreams are born
out of space and time.

But our wish for you
is that your birthday be filled
with dreams that come true.
The magic for us—is having you!

HAPPY BIRTHDAY, ANTHONY!

HAPPY BIRTHDAY, ETHAN

It's NUMBER ONE!
Let's celebrate . . .
eight tiny little teeth
in a smile so-o-o-o sweet;
your eyes . . . intent,
as they gaze into mine,
turning my face around and around
in study.
What deep, deep thoughts
lie behind?

HAPPY BIRTHDAY, ELI

Today you're one!
Like a little robot
you totter around,
arms outstretched.
Nothing's safe
from your little hands.
And . . . you now have teeth;
four's the count.
It took so-o-o-o long, but,

OH! THAT SMILE!

I'M GONNA KEEP GOING

When our little grandson, Anthony, celebrated his third birthday, he and his mother and father came to our house for dinner, birthday cake, and presents.

Anthony loved "Thomas the Train," a wooden train set, complete with wooden tracks, small wooden engines, and all kinds of accessories. One could purchase a minimal amount, or put lots of money into it. Anthony had the basics—a small amount of track, a Thomas engine, a conductor engine, and another engine called Percy. His mother cued us in that we could really please him if we were to give him a Thomas the Train turntable. That, we decided, would be our gift for him.

That evening, after dinner and birthday cake, Anthony opened his gifts. When he opened ours, he became very excited. "It's the turntable!" he exclaimed. Refusing to put it down, he turned to his mother and said, "Momma, let's go home now."

"But you haven't opened all your presents," his mother replied. With a little reluctance, Anthony put his turntable down and turned back to the rest of his gifts, while keeping a close eye on the turntable.

When Anthony reached the last gift and tore off the paper, his face lit up. "It's the tunnel!" he shouted. That was also something he had been wishing for. He tucked the turntable under one arm, and holding the tunnel with both hands, he said, "Momma, I'm ready to go home now."

"In a few minutes," she replied.

Anthony turned and walked toward the door which leads to the garage. About halfway through the kitchen, he said loudly, "I'm going!"

We all sat and watched. When he reached the door, which was locked and which he wasn't able to unlock, he stopped, looked up at the door, looked back at us and said, "I'm gonna keep going!"

He was so cute and so funny, but it was his excitement, his eagerness, his determination—to get home and play with his new Thomas the Train accessories—that impressed me most.

—⚹—

Lord, grant that we may have such enthusiasm,
such eagerness and determination to pursue the goals
you set for us . . . even through locked doors!

Whatsoever thy hand findeth to do,
do it with thy might.
(Ecclesiastes 9:10a KJV)

I WANT TO DANCE
WITH THE PRINCESS

It was our church's 150th anniversary. Part of the weekend celebration was to hold an open house in each of the three buildings that had served as our church home.

The first church home, built in 1852, was a beautiful two-story building in the center of town. In 1897, when the church had outgrown the building, it was purchased by a prominent and prestigious women's club. Kept in good condition, the historic old building is still owned today by the women of the club and used for their twice-monthly meetings and other functions.

As a member of the church and also the women's club that owns the building, I agreed to act as hostess at the clubhouse, and to dress in colonial costume such as the women wore in the 1800s. My colonial gown was a beautiful pale blue silk, trimmed with lace along the neckline and the three-quarter length sleeves, with a long, full skirt flowing from the tight-fitting waist to the floor. The skirt was further enhanced by beautiful flounces on each side. As hostess, my duty was to greet everyone who entered, relate the history of the building, and show the visitors around.

At one point during the open house, I was very pleased to see a friend from the church, accompanied by her daughter and two small granddaughters, come to see the building. I showed them around the first floor and then took them upstairs. After giving a brief explanation of the church's use of the building, I left them to browse on their own and went back downstairs. Shortly after, they came down. As they were saying goodbye, the oldest granddaughter, who was about four years old, whispered in her mother's ear. Her mother glanced at me and smiled. "She wants to dance with the princess."

What a pleasant surprise! In this little girl's mind, I was a princess! Me . . . a princess! I was so pleased and, of course, I had to dance with the little girl, even if it was only to swirl around the room for a few minutes. That incident made the weekend one I will never forget. Me . . . a princess!

In thinking about the incident later, and about kings and queens, princes and princesses, I realized that in a way, I am a princess. All those who believe in the Lord and have chosen to follow His teachings are considered to be His sons and daughters. There is no higher authority—He is the King. And that makes me—truly a princess!

I thank that little child for making God's teachings come alive for me that day in such a beautiful, innocent, childlike fashion. I will forever now think of myself as a princess, and hopefully, with God's help, conduct myself as one.

—⚭—

Thus saith the Lord . . .
I am the Lord, your Holy One,
the creator of Israel, your King.
(Isaiah 43:14–15 KJV)

What is man, that thou art mindful of him?
And the son of man, that thou visitest him?
For thou hast made him a little lower than the angels,
and hast crowned him with glory and honour.
(Psalm 8:4–5 KJV)

WHERE WE GOING, DAD?

When they were four, our twin grandsons Ethan and Eli were enrolled in preschool. Before school started that year, the boys were required to have blood tests to check for lead content. Now, both boys had had shots before, but no blood tests. The procedure required that a needle be inserted into the arm, inside the elbow, with blood drawn into a vial, similar to blood tests for adults. The only difference is that, for a child, the needle and vial are smaller. Knowing this was going to be a totally new and traumatic experience for the boys, both parents accompanied them to the lab. And wisely, they didn't tell them what was going to happen.

It was decided Ethan should go first. While Dad took Ethan down the hall to the room for the blood tests, Mom tried to keep Eli occupied in the waiting room. After inspecting everything in the room, they began to explore the outside, identifying the objects on the lawn. In a few minutes, just as she expected, Mom recognized Ethan's cries of pain and anguish, echoing down the long hallway. But Eli didn't notice.

Soon Dad was back with Ethan, who, still sniffling, flew to his mother, hiding his face against her legs. Now it was Eli's turn and Dad immediately took his little hand and they started down the hallway.

"Where we going, Dad?" Eli's words were loud and clear.

Dad apparently did not answer because, once again, the question came, "Where we going, Dad?" And then, "Dad, I don't think I want to go back here."

But Dad, being the loving father that he is, knowing that the blood test was necessary and for Eli's good, held tightly to his little hand and they continued on their way. Before long, Eli's cries of pain and anguish could be heard, echoing down the hallway. Needless to say, both boys survived and were none the worse for the experience. And the results were good—no lead content was found in their blood.

At times, aren't we like little Eli when we are faced with something we sense is going to be unpleasant? Don't we balk, and ask the Lord to please correct the situation, or take it away? Don't we, like little Eli, find ourselves saying, "Lord, I don't think I want to go back here"?

Nevertheless, we, too, will find that our loving heavenly Father, who has a divine plan for each of our lives, will "hold tightly to our hand" and lead us steadily onward, knowing that the experience is necessary and for our good. For such great love, let us give thanks.

—〰—

For I know the plans I have for you, says the Lord,
plans for welfare, and not for evil,
to give you a future and a hope.
(Jeremiah 29:11 RSV)

WALKING IN FAITH

By faith, Abraham . . .
went out, not knowing whither he went.
(Hebrews 11:8 KJV)

Can I do this? It's a huge responsibility. What if I fail? I was struggling still, after many days, with a decision that had consumed my thoughts and prayers.

Recently, I had been asked to serve in a leadership position in which I would be working with many other women, involving a lot of travel over two states, Delaware and Pennsylvania. It was a three-year commitment, and seemed a huge task—one that I wasn't sure I could handle. And so, I prayed and I struggled with the decision.

And then, I was reminded of Abraham in the Bible. Abraham, the great patriarch and father of many nations, had great faith and trust in God. He was asked to uproot— his family, his belongings, everything—and to set out at God's command to move. Where? He did not know where he was to go. But, he went. Such faith, such trust—so vital in our relationship with the Lord.

I realized then that we, like Abraham, when faced with a difficult journey (or task), can place our faith, our trust, our hand in God's hand, and let Him lead. Then, our destination is sure.

AT THE ZOO

Together they walk,
small hand in large,
stride matched to stride;
the large, the small,
the short, the tall,
the man, the child.

Past iron-barred cages
where monkeys stare,
and giant bears sit unperturbed
by mammoth hunks of granite.
Secure the child,
small hand held tight,
innocence trusting.
Nonchalant the man,
having faced life's "lions"
and walked away,
he guards the charge that's his.

Though time will change
the measured steps,
the strength of hand,
the child to man,
protected to protector,
the bond will hold.

Grandfather, grandson.

SEEING WITH NEW EYES

That the God of our Lord Jesus Christ,
the Father of glory,
may give unto you the spirit of wisdom
and revelation in the knowledge of him:
The eyes of your understanding being enlightened.
(Ephesians 1:17–18a KJV)

We have been blessed with three wonderful grandsons: Anthony and the twins, Ethan and Eli. One morning when the twins were five, Ethan went with his dad to the store. He had saved his money and had been given permission to buy a limited number of collectible Yu-Gi-Oh cards. Yu-Gi-Oh was one of the animated cartoon figures he liked to watch on children's television.

Ethan was excited, but when he saw all the many cards that were available, he wanted to purchase all of the series. Dad called home so that Ethan could check with his mother. "Absolutely not!" she said. "Only what we agreed upon." So Ethan, unhappy, went home with a long face.

Later that afternoon, Dad was working in the yard when Ethan approached. "Dad," he said, "if you could have anything you wanted, what would you choose?"

After a little thought, Dad replied, "Well, I think I would like a new boat . . ."

"If I could have anything I wanted, I would choose more Yu-Gi-Oh cards," Ethan said. Then, after a brief pause, "Dad, let's make a deal. You can get a new boat, and I can get more Yu-Gi-Oh cards." He stood still for just a moment, then frowned. "Dad, let's make another deal. Let's not tell Mommy. Okay?"

Now, Ethan had obviously been doing a lot of thinking. Only five years old, he was growing and maturing, learning about life and about people—and he was beginning to reason. One might say he was beginning to "see with new eyes." And probably, at some point, we all begin to "see with new eyes."

Those who are fitted with eyeglasses or contact lenses, and those who have had cataract removal or corneal transplants, see with new eyes. It could also be said of those who undergo an experience that changes them or their lives, that they, too, begin to see with new eyes.

In the Bible, we have the story of Saul, renowned persecutor of the early Christians. Once, on his way to Damascus, Saul had an experience in which he was blinded for three days, and when his sight was restored, he began to see things in a different way than ever before. It was in this experience on the road to Damascus that Saul met the Christ. After this, his name was changed to Paul, and instead of persecuting Christians, he became their friend and helper. He became a worker for the Lord, a great preacher and missionary.

Later, in a letter to the church at Ephesus, Paul wrote, "I pray . . . that the eyes of your heart may be enlightened." He could have added "as mine have been," for Paul had begun to "see with new eyes." He had begun to see as Jesus did—through eyes of love and compassion.

—∾—

May the eyes of your heart (and mine) be enlightened. May we all see as Jesus saw.

The Waiting Room

It's nice, Lord,
this quiet room,
disturbed only by the rustle
of magazine pages
turned by those who wait.

Through the window,
magnolia leaves sway gently
in the afternoon breeze.
Above, cotton ball clouds
slide slowly
across the wide blue
in the bright commanding light
of the sun.

A reminder . . .
that your Spirit guides,
directs,
and fills my heart
as I listen for *Your* call
in the waiting room of life.

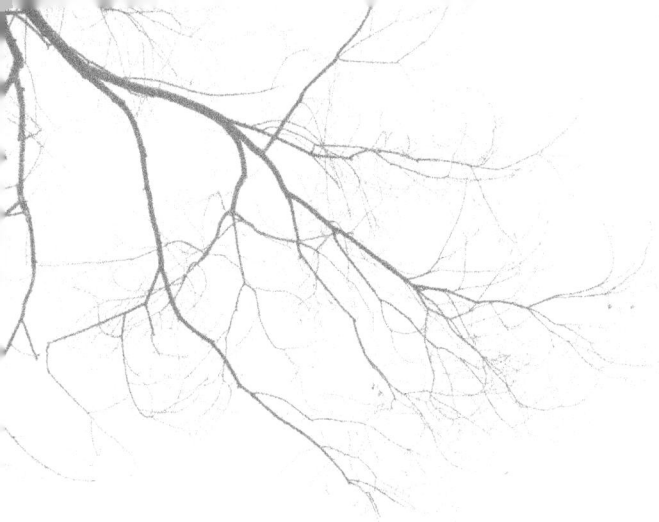

Leafless Winter

—⚏—

Winter

A Tiime for Rest,
Evaluation,
And Preparation
For
A New Beginning

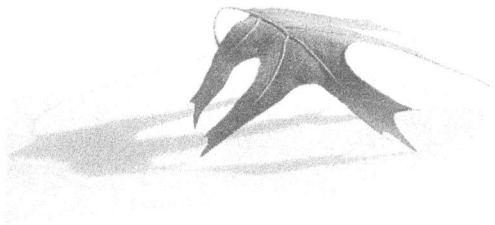

THE LATTER YEARS

Much like the winter season
are the latter years of one's life.
In winter, the trees stand bare,
stripped of their covering of leaves.
Once signs of spring, new life,
freshness and youth,
leaves later become marks of growth,
maturity, and fruit for
the harvest; and then,
they fall from the tree.

So it is in the latter years of our lives . . .
Signs of our spring,
our youth, have changed,
through growth, maturing, and age.
Finally, we, like the trees, stand bare;
our winter has come.

But, winter has its beauty, its purpose,
as God has planned.
Beneath the bleakness,
the lack of evidence of verdant growth,
seeds of new life are being nurtured
and prepared—
to burst forth
when the season is right.

He hath made every thing beautiful in his time: . . .
(Ecclesiastes 3:11 KJV)

—⁘—

Lord, thank You for opening my eyes
to the beauty of winter.

January Sand

(to a seagull)

—⚡—

What are you thinking, little friend?
Safe behind the fence you stand.
Is that your ocean?
Is this your sand?

Silver ripples, cold blue water,
ships distant against the sky;
fellow seagulls circle, hovering,
sound their melancholy cry.

A lonely couple, arms entwined,
explore the shifting, curving shore;
seeking Neptune's salty secrets
cast aside by winter storms.

Seashells whisper, "You're intruding;"
driftwood, seaweed, block the way.
Alone, you hold your post, undaunted;
so disapproving, unafraid.

The shore is yours, now, little friend,
volunteer-watchman of the tides;
for just a while, 'til winter's end,
enjoy the beach, the breeze, the sand.

EVERYWHERE, CHRISTMAS

—◦◦◦—

I n his poem, "A Christmas Carol," Phillips Brooks describes Christmas with these words: "Everywhere, everywhere, Christmas tonight." Most would agree that this beloved holiday, coming at the beginning of the winter season, does seem to be everywhere. Christmas has its own special aliveness, like the wind blowing over the earth, hidden in all the decorations, in the sights and sounds of the season. Phillips Brooks' words inspired me to write the following poem.

EVERYWHERE, CHRISTMAS

Hand bells ring;
pipe organs swell their music
loud and clear;
church choirs sing out, and children shout,
"Christmas time is here!"
Streets are lit with tiny lights, all twinkling red and green;
wreaths with bows, and Christmas trees
can everywhere be seen.

Stores are full and shoppers rush,
their goods to price, and choose that perfect gift
for Uncle Jim, Aunt Sue, and Cousin Ruth.
Lines are long, smiles turn to frowns;
tired patrons wait, and smart,
while the angel beckons
from the manger scene,
"Is it Christmas in your heart?"

At Christmas time, the holiday glow
is beautiful to see . . . but,
has our hearing dulled and our eyesight dimmed
to the message Christmas brings?
Of that holy night when the angels sang,
their good news to impart,
of the Christ Child born in Bethlehem . . .
Let it be Christmas in your heart.

—⚉—

And the angel said unto them, Fear not;
for behold, I bring you good tidings
of great joy, which shall be to all people.
For unto you is born this day
in the city of David,
a Saviour, which is Christ the Lord.
(Luke 2:10–11 KJV)

BLESS ME, TOO, O MY FATHER

It was Anthony's tenth birthday. Not long after the family arrived at our house for the celebration, one of the twins, five-year-old Ethan, sidled over to where I was sitting. He had seen his older brother's birthday gift, wrapped and placed on the hearth in the family room.

"Mom-Mom," Ethan said, his hazel eyes looking hopefully into mine, "Do you have some more presents someplace?"

Now, it doesn't take a genius to determine that Ethan was really asking if we had a gift for him. Matter of fact, we did; however, the twins were not to receive their gifts until Anthony had opened his. So I skirted around the issue without giving him a direct answer. Needless to say, he was a very happy little boy later—with a gift in his hand.

This incident reminded me of another set of twins in the Bible, Esau and Jacob, and how Esau, the older, sold his birthright to Jacob for a bowl of stew. Later, when Esau went to receive his blessing from his father, Isaac, he discovered the blessing had already been given to Jacob. Esau's poignant cry, "Bless me, too, O my father," is hard to forget.

We all like to receive gifts, like little Ethan on his brother's birthday; and we all hope to be blessed by God, our heavenly Father. Throughout the Bible, we see evidence of God's great love for us and His desire to bless us. Psalm 37:4 (KJV) reads, "Delight thyself also in the Lord; and He shall give thee the desires of thine heart." What He asks of us, though, is that we love Him in return, obey His commandments, and believe in His Son, Jesus Christ—His greatest gift of all.

—⚹—

May Esau's cry be yours and mine . . .
"Bless me, too, O my Father."
(see Genesis 27:34)

HOLY JOES

One evening, I attended a church service with a friend. While waiting for the service to begin, I leaned over to my friend and whispered, "Do you realize this is the fourth prayer service we have attended in four days?"

My friend smiled and said, "We will have to be careful—we don't want to become known as 'Holy Joes.'"

I laughed, of course, and so did my friend. I laughed, not only because it was a humorous remark, but also because of the incongruity, with all of my imperfections, to think that I could ever be deserving of the label "holy." However, in thinking about my friend's comment later, would it be so bad to be labeled a "Holy Joe," just because one attends prayer meetings often and is known as one who prays?

The Bible tells us to pray. Examples of this include the following: *Men ought always to pray.* (Luke 18:1 KJV); *Pray without ceasing* (1 Thessalonians 5:17 KJV); *Be careful for nothing; but in everything by prayer and supplication with thanksgiving let your requests be made known unto God* (Philippians 4:6 KJV).

The Bible not only tells us to pray, it also gives examples of prayer and of individuals who were known as men or women of prayer. Abraham was a man of prayer, and he became the father of many nations. Elijah prayed, and it did not rain for three years and six months. He prayed again and the rain fell. Hannah prayed fervently for a child, and the Lord gave her a son, Samuel. Jesus prayed, the disciples watched and said, "Lord, teach us to pray."

What is prayer but time spent in the Lord's presence, communing with Him, talking with Him, listening for His reply, and learning of Him—His will and His way? In her book, *Moments That Matter*, Catherine Marshall discusses the importance of prayer. She says that when Jesus prayed, God had thrilling secrets to share with Him, exciting new ideas to give to Him, much to teach Him. I like to think that God has thrilling secrets to share with me, too—that He is waiting to share new ideas and new concepts with me—that He has much to teach me.

Come, be a "Holy Joe" with me!

HICKORY, DICKORY, DOCK
THE MOUSE RAN UP THE CLOCK

—⚬—

When I was a child,
hot lazy summers
seemed to last forever.
The best day of the year,
except for Christmas Day,
was the last day of school.

Seems strange,
how summers have shortened
now that I am older,
though school still ends in June,
or thereabouts,
and then begins again
in August or September.

Today, however,
summer's no sooner started
than it's ended.
But the clock ticks steadily;
sixty minutes an hour,
twenty-four hours a day,
seven days a week,
four weeks a month,
twelve months a year.

Could it be . . .
the mouse runs more slowly now?

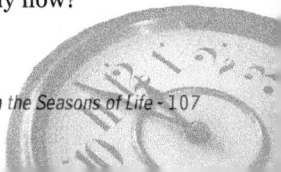

HOLD ON TIGHT

When our twin grandsons, Ethan and Eli, were toddlers, I was usually given charge of Ethan when we would go out. This meant being the one to hold his hand while walking down the street or wandering around inside a store, watching over him no matter what we were doing. Always, I would take his little hand in mine and say, "Now, Ethan, hold on tight to Mom-Mom's hand."

However, after one or two outings with the boys, it didn't take long for me to realize it wasn't Ethan who was holding on tight—it was the other way around. Ethan always wanted to let go, to pull away, to run ahead. It was Mom-Mom who was holding on tight. I held his little hand as tightly as I could, lest he let go and trip and fall—or even worse, run into the street and get hit by a car.

This simple incident helped me to realize that in those times of stress in our lives when we need the Lord's help— to protect, to heal, to help us through a difficult situation—

it is not we who are holding on tightly to God's hand, it is the other way around. It is He who has our hand placed firmly in His, holding tight, so that we cannot pull away, or run ahead, or trip and fall. It is He who will see that we make it safely to the place He would have us go.

—⁊⁊⁊—

The steps of a good man are ordered by the Lord:
and he delighteth in his way.
Though he fall, he shall not be utterly cast down:
for the Lord upholdeth him with his hand.
(Psalm 37:23–24 KJV)

WHAT IS LONELY?

The babble of a brook
in silent woods;
the rustle of the wind in the treetops;
a country road in the noonday sun
and no one sees the traveler.

A wobbly highchair
on an attic floor;
an earless teddy bear,
a worn-out glove;
echoes of voices once happy at play,
and only the heart hears the laughter.

The click of the phone
across many miles;
an empty mailbox
at the end of the day;
on New Year's eve, a lonely bed;
and no one hears the heart break.

SECURITY

In the book, *The Demi-Gods*, James Stephens remarks, "Women and birds are able to see without turning their heads, and that is indeed a necessary provision, for they are both surrounded by enemies."

Now I think Stephens was being a little facetious. Granted, he may have a point in that women are able to see without turning their heads, but—surrounded by enemies? That is a provocative thought. And it could be true—if not for all women, at least for some, somewhere in this vast universe. However, it does point out the importance of security for all of us.

Research shows that billions of dollars are spent in America each year on security-related products and services, from locks to alarm systems to guards. That says a lot about how secure we Americans feel. It seems safe to say our security keeps dwindling each day with the increased acts of violence and crime that are reported—and especially with the ever-present danger of identity theft and even acts of terror. And so, our fears balloon. The fact is that crime has increased to alarming proportions, and so has our need for security.

Security comes in many forms. It might be in the uniformed presence of law enforcement, an alarm system, bars on one's windows, or in carrying a gun; but there are other kinds of security. One's security might lie in being in familiar surroundings, having set routines, observing established traditions and customs. For some, though, the greatest security lies in an unshakeable faith and trust in God and the promises found in His Word, such as this:

> *In peace I will both lie down and sleep;*
> *for thou alone, O Lord,*
> *makest me dwell in safety.*
> (Psalm 4:8 RSV)

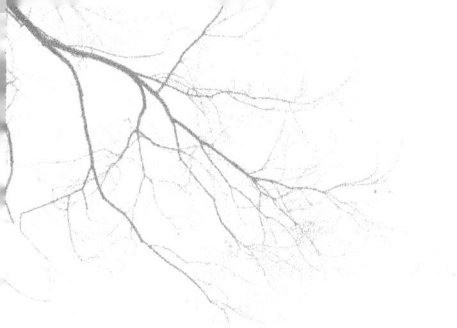

Amazing Grace

*For God so loved the world,
that he gave his only begotten son,
that whosoever believeth in Him
should not perish, but have everlasting life.*
(John 3:16 KJV)

I looked around at the other members of the Sunday school class. All were dear friends, most of whom I had known for many years. And all were followers of Christ.

We had been discussing the controversy in the world concerning Jesus. Yes, we all agreed, controversy still exists today, just as it did when He walked the earth. Today, just as then, to some He is the Christ, the Savior of the world; to some just a prophet; to others, merely a good man; and some do not know Him at all.

I pondered our sinful world—a world in which biblical principles, God's teachings, even God himself, are being compromised and ruled unconstitutional. A world in which our long-established God-given ordinances, such as marriage, are being questioned; abortion is legalized, sex scandals in high places of authority continually come to light, and immorality and self-satisfaction seem to be the rule. Yet, here we were, a small group, bound together in Christ, secure in our faith in God and firm in our assurance of eternal life through Christ. How had it happened that we were here—that I was here—and not *out there*?

Suddenly, God's grace took on new meaning. I, a sinner, could so easily have been "out there" in the world. But, the Bible tells us that *God our Saviour . . . will have all men to be saved, and to come unto the knowledge of the truth* (1 Timothy 2:3–4 KJV). He leaves no stone unturned in His attempts to reach us and draw us unto Himself. I was here, we were here, in that Sunday school room that morning because we had heard God's voice, and had chosen to believe in His son, Jesus Christ, and to trust in Him. We were where we were by the grace of God. *And only by His grace.*

Aftermath

Then shall the dust return to the earth as it was:
and the spirit shall return unto God who gave it.
(Ecclesiastes 12:7 KJV)

At the site of the accident, the man and woman got out of their van and walked slowly across the grass, marred by deep ruts. The accident had happened near my home, forty-eight hours earlier, about two o'clock in the morning. One of the two vehicles involved, after leaving the highway, struck several huge old trees with such force the trees had broken in two. The driver and his passenger, both young men, were killed.

One of the young men was soon to have been married. Just moments before, he and his friend had been to a bachelor party, given in honor of the bridegroom. But now, for those two young men, all vital signs had been extinguished, all hopes and dreams were gone.

My heart filled with sadness as I watched the woman walk up to one of the trees, kneel, and place two bouquets of flowers at the foot of the tree. Then she leaned against the tree, her head on her arm, and I could see that she was sobbing. I could only pray for the man and the woman in their grief—and hope that the two young men had known the Lord.

—⚉—

For I am persuaded,
that neither death,
nor life,
nor angels,
nor principalities,
nor powers,
nor things present,
nor things to come,
Nor height,
nor depth,
nor any other creature,
shall be able to separate us from the love of God,
which is in Christ Jesus our Lord.
(Romans 8:38–39 KJV)

Printed previously in *On the Way with American Baptist Women*, Spring/Summer 2002

IN SILHOUETTE

When winter comes
and snowflakes fall,
gentle
to the ground,
I will remember
this friend of mine.

Her love for life,
daughter, friends;
how she loved to laugh,
how she loved to dine.

I will recall
a wedding in June,
her daughter, our son;
another year, another room,
birthday surprise,
her tear-filled eyes.

Independent, strong,
she fought for her rights,
for her daughter,
for life;
but her winter came.

So when robins nest in springtime,
in summer's fragrant rose,
in the golden mums of autumn,
and winter's gentle snow,
Aline
I will remember.

WHAT ARE YOU LEAVING BEHIND?

My father-in-law is gone now, but there were times when we would go to visit that he would hurry upstairs to bring down memorabilia for us to see. On one such occasion, he came down with a Bible, which he said was about 100 years old.

Inside that century-old Bible, I found a scrap of paper. It appeared to be a sheet of paper from a writing tablet, lined and yellowed with age. There was writing on the paper, apparently a verse from a poem, which read:

> *He is coming Old Earth;*
> *He is coming tonight,*
> *To a world that is weary and worn.*

Those words and the fact that they had been left behind by someone many, many years ago—maybe even a hundred years ago—impressed me very much. I considered the context and the fact that they were left in a Bible. *They probably refer to Jesus, the Christ Child, and they were probably used in a Christmas program.* The description of the world amazed me. It could easily have referred to our present twenty-first century world, definitely one that is even more weary and worn than it was those many years ago. And definitely one in need of a Savior. Nevertheless, those words carried a message, and they told me something about the person who left them in that Bible.

I had no idea who the person was, and neither did my father-in-law. However, we could tell what kind of person he or she was from that scrap of paper. He or she was evidently someone who knew about Christ; someone who attended church and took part in church activities. That scrap of paper bore a Christian witness, even after all the years that had passed. Those things we do, those parts of ourselves that we leave behind, tell who we are.

What are you leaving behind? What part of yourself that tells who you are—whose you are—will someone find tomorrow, next week, next year, even years from now? It could be a scrap of paper containing words about Christ, stuffed in a drawer, a book, or perhaps a Bible. It could be an act of kindness, or a difficult job well done. On the other hand, it might be a thoughtless deed, or words expressed in anger. These are the things the world sees and measures.

—∿—

You will know them by their fruits.
Are grapes gathered from thorns, or figs from thistles?
(Matthew 7:16 RSV)

Bright Spots

Once at a writer's conference in Green Lake, Wisconsin, I participated in a poetry workshop. The workshop was held down in the woods in an old house reserved only for writers attending the conference.

One morning, following a terrific electrical storm, as I stood in the kitchen during morning break, I heard a bird singing. The sound was very loud and very close. Stepping to the screen door, I looked outside, and there on the small porch outside the kitchen was a beautiful brown wood thrush, perched on the beam under the ceiling. He was about three feet away, and it was as though he was singing his song just for me. I could only stand motionless, spellbound—it was beautiful. The sound was guttural, coming from deep in his throat, rising higher and higher; and he sang his song over and over. It was a refresher for my faith, a reminder that God, Creator of the Universe and everything within, was there. I considered it a special gift from God.

We all need such bright spots in our lives—sometimes in the worst kind of way. Our lives can become difficult, hectic, dreary, sometimes filled with anxiety and worry. During times such as these we need bright spots, those extremely impressive experiences that cheer us and lift our spirits and remind us of God—that He cares and that He is near. It could be the sight of a cardinal in the midst of the snow of December; it might be the beauty of a tree-lined street in the fall with the trees ablaze with color; it might be a gaggle of snow geese with their mournful, but beautiful, cry as they pass overhead; or it could be a word softly spoken. Bright spots come in many forms.

A year or so following the incident at Green Lake, my husband was diagnosed with cancer, resulting in four surgeries, and finally removal of his bladder. Our lives were completely altered, and during the following years, bright spots were very much needed as we struggled to adjust to the change and to my husband's bouts of severe clinical depression. During this time, those special gifts from God—those bright spots—brightened my days and reminded me of God's presence with us.

With grateful hearts, especially during those times when our hearts cry out, "God, where are you?" let us watch for those bright spots the Lord sends into our lives. Let us watch for those times when He says, "Hey, it's Me, God! I'm right here with you." And let us give thanks.

—∿—

I will not leave you comfortless;
I will come to you.

He that hath my commandments,
and keepeth them, he it is that loveth me:
and he that loveth me shall be loved of my Father,
and I will love him,
and will manifest myself to him.

(John 14:18, 21 KJV)

BRIGHT SPOTS

Tiny purple flowers
in a purple pot
and another the same.
Refreshing,
above the drab brown
of the cabinet;
like the song of the thrush
after the storm.

He was outside the kitchen,
perched on a beam
under the ceiling.
From deep in his throat
beautiful music swelled,
as over and over
he sang his song.

God-gifts.

—〰—

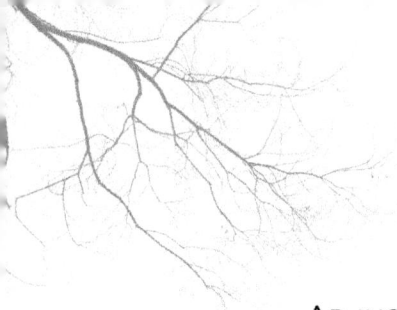

ADJUSTING

I'm learning to live with the loneliness;
the empty bed at night,
the empty chair across the table,
and the quiet sound of nothingness
where once was life and light.

But there are times when the solitary
cuts like a knife,
and I cannot help but unlock the door
of remembering;
knowing full well the pain that will come
in seeing your smile,
and hearing your voice,
and imagining your arms holding me tight,
safe, protected, loved.

If only . . .
If only the moment could last.
But then, you're gone,
and I'm left alone in my room,
full, yet empty.

Some Trust in Chariots

"Oh, no," I cried, glancing at the clock. "It's almost midnight, I've got to go to bed! I have to be at the hospital by six in the morning." My thoughts were churning, just as my nerves had been doing all day. Two weeks earlier, I had been diagnosed with invasive breast cancer and was scheduled for surgery. I picked up my Bible, feeling a great need to sense God's presence—tonight, especially. I had felt so alone this past year since my husband's death.

"Lord, I'm just going to read one of the Psalms," I prayed quietly, "and then go to bed." Opening my Bible, I glanced down at the page. I had opened to Psalm 20, and a word in the first verse caught my attention: *May the Lord answer you when you are in distress*. Distress! I was certainly in distress tonight.

I had been told I would be in the hospital most of the day, since there were several procedures that were necessary, including the lumpectomy to remove the cancer and any affected lymph nodes.

Quite anxious about everything, I continued reading. "Amen," I whispered as I read verse 7:

> *Some trust in chariots and some in horses,*
> *but we trust in the name*
> *of the Lord our God.*
> *(Psalm 20:7 NIV)*

"My trust is definitely in you, Lord." I read the psalm again and closed my Bible.

At the hospital the next morning, after the preliminary tasks were taken care of, I was assigned to a bed in Day Surgery. I looked around.

There's Peggy and Dan! I wonder why they're here. I haven't seen them since they left the church. Was it five— or six—years ago?

Peggy looked surprised to see me, and in a few minutes was at my bedside.

"Hello," she said. "What are you doing here?"

As I explained, shock registered in her brown eyes, slid down her face, and erased her smile, but not her friendly, caring manner. She chatted cheerfully with me for about thirty minutes. "I'll be back," she said, when she left.

And she did return, accompanied by the assistant pastor from her church, whom I had not met before. They stayed only a few minutes, and prayed with me before they left. Later, she stopped by again. Taking my hand, she whispered, "Dan's tests are finished and we're leaving. But I wanted to say goodbye and to wish you well." Her kindness meant so much to me.

About 4:00 p.m., the grueling day was over. My daughter Lisa had taken the afternoon off from her job to come down and drive me to her home for a few days. "The doctor's report was really good, Mom. How do you feel?"

"Tired. But so glad it's over. All those needles, the X-rays, the special markings, and having to lie perfectly still under that special lamp while they traced the dye through the lymph system. I thought that would never end. And then, there were those seven needles they used to insert the dye—without numbing—that was worse. I hope I never have to go through that again. But Rosie was there. Rosie was the nurse who held my hand."

About an hour later, the forty-mile drive behind us, I was ready for bed. Remembering how comforting Psalm 20 had been the night before, I wanted to read it again. But when I reached the second verse, I stopped—and simply stared at the words:

May he send you help from the sanctuary
and grant you support from Zion
(Psalm 20:2 NIV).

And just then, the Lord said to me, "Isn't that what I did for you today?"

Memories of the morning rushed into my head. Peggy and Dan were there! And Peggy's pastor—and he prayed for me! That was "help from the sanctuary!"

Stunned, my heart began to beat a little faster. *Lord, that's exactly what you did! You were telling me last night in this Psalm what you were going to do today. You want me to know you've been with me every moment.*

I closed my eyes, engulfed by a tidal wave of gratitude and praise for the wonderful, loving, living God who is ours. *Thank You, Lord. You did this for me—for me!*

At that moment I knew—without a doubt—that whatever the future holds, I will not face it alone. Truly, I can say with the psalmist,

> *"Some trust in chariots and some in horses,*
> *but [I] will trust in the Lord my God forever."*
> (Psalm 20:7 NIV, personalized)

WINTER WAIT

Who does not love to see the leaves
begin to bud on the branch of a tree?

A welcome sight for sure,
after a season of frost and snow.

'Tis the promise of spring
long waited for

through cold winter nights,
warmed by the fire

of the hearth
and the heart.

For 'tis the heart that knows . . .

with winter's end
comes spring.

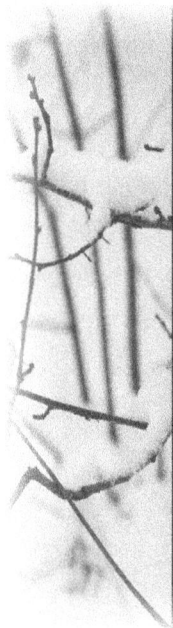

TO EVERY

THING THERE IS

A SEASON,

AND

A TIME TO EVERY PURPOSE

UNDER THE HEAVEN.

(Ecclesiastes 3:1 KJV,
The Guideposts Parallel Bible)

In Grateful
Appreciation

—◦—

First to God, the giver of all good gifts,
and then to my beloved husband,
my greatest fan and most severe critic,
who will not see the finished product . . .
except from above.

I am especially grateful to
my family for being my inspiration;
to Pastor Roland G. Coon of Calvary,
for his review and kind words of endorsement;
and to all who offered
words of encouragement
along the way.

I would be remiss not to express appreciation
to Fruitbearer Publishing LLC;
to Wilma Caraway and Melissa Peitsh
for the hours they spent refining the manuscript;
and, most important, to Candy Abbott,
not only for being my publisher and mentor
but also a true and loving friend.

And a special thank you to my daughter Lisa
who lovingly and patiently
kept me on course.

MARY EMMA TISINGER

Southern-born, from the foot-hills of the North Carolina mountains, Mary Emma now calls the flatlands of Delaware home. Always a lover of words, she writes poetry, fiction, and non-fiction, and is currently authoring a newsletter. She is a member of the Academy of American Poets, Delmarva Christian Writers' Fellowship, and the Eastern Shore Writers Association. Her poetry and other writings have appeared in a variety of magazines, publications, and books.

ORDER INFO

—*m*—

Through the Leaves that Fall

Available online
or from your favorite bookseller

For autographed books
or to schedule speaking engagements,
contact the author at:

MaryEmmaT@verizon.net
302.697.2263

For bulk discounts contact:

Fruitbearer Publishing, LLC
P. O. Box 777, Georgetown, DE 19947
302.856.6649 • FAX 302.856.7742
info@fruitbearer.com • www.fruitbearer.com

www.ingramcontent.com/pod-product-compliance
Lightning Source LLC
Chambersburg PA
CBHW060324050426
42449CB00011B/2645